"WAIT"

(The Importance of You)

By

Mozell L. Bryant

To God Be All The Glory

A Must Read For Pre-Teens and Young Adults

Table of Contents

Author's Biography

Introduction

Merriam Webster Definitions

Making Good Choices

Get To Know You

Integrity Is Key

Time Is On Your Side

Your Purpose

You Need Wisdom

You Decide

Know You

Know Who You Are

You

You and School

You and God

A Feeling of Void In Your Life

Don't Be Fooled

Summary

Sources of References

Author's Biography

My name is Mozell Smiley-Bryant. I was born in the country (Dade City). I was born number three out of ten children. I have always had a deep love for children even as a child. I was an introvert as a child. I try to inspire children to be the best that they can be. I wrote many short books and poems over the years about children as I was growing up and they were inadvertently tossed. I have two Published poems about children. I have worked with children for over 50 years in churches (I served as Youth Coordinator, Youth Counsellor, Tutored, Youth Praise, Mime and Drill Team Instructor.); school (Tutored and Speaker) and worked in many other areas in day cares and in the community. I have learned many things over the years and gained insight into many unspoken words of the young. God inspired me to start writing to children to share the wisdom I've gained with them and about them. I hope you enjoy the insights. This is just the beginning. There will be many more books to come.

God bless you and thank you for taking time to read and hopefully share with others. Love you,

Introduction

First, giving glory, honor and praises to my Savior, Jesus Christ. For it is with Him and through Him that I have my being. God is so Awesome!

This book speaks to young people that have concerns, questions, issues, problems and to some that feel they have nowhere to turn. Every child is not fortunate to have someone to listen, understand and give an unbiased answer. Children seek first an attentive ear. Someone that will take time out and listen to what they are saying! Sometimes it might not make any sense to an adult but listen, you will probably figure out what they are trying to ask or say! Listen so you get to know your child and what's on their mind. Second, be truthful about whatever it is. They will check it out sooner or later. Third, spend some quality time with them. That's when you can pour wisdom and knowledge into them. Because then you will not give rush answers! They know the difference! Believe me!

I hope to give insight into young people about who they are and what they should stand for. Hope you enjoy!

MERRIAM WEBSTER DEFINITIONS

Definition of WAIT
Transitive verb - to stay in place in expectation of; Intransitive verb - to remain stationary in readiness or expectation; to look forward expectantly; to hold back expectantly.

Definition of SEEK
transitive verb -to resort to; to go in search of; look for; to try to discover; to ask for/request; seeks advice; to try to acquire or gain; to make an attempt/try; intransitive verb: to make a search or inquiry;

Definition of RELATIONSHIP
The state of being related or interrelated; the relation connecting or binding participants in a relationship: passionate attachment

Definition of INTEGRITY
Firm adherence to a code of especially moral or artistic values: INCORRUPTIBILITY; an unimpaired condition/SOUNDNESS; the quality or state of being complete or undivided/COMPLETENESS; the quality of being honest and fair; the state of being complete or whole.

Definition of PURPOSE
something set up as an object or end to be attained; INTENTION; RESOLUTION, DETERMINATION; a subject under discussion or an action in course of execution; by intent: INTENTIONALLY; the reason why something is done or used; the aim or intention of something; the feeling of being determined to do or achieve something; the aim or goal of a person: what a person is trying to do, become, etc.

Definition of CHOICE
the act of choosing: SELECTION; power of choosing: OPTION; the best part; a person or thing chosen; care in selecting; to be preferred; the act of choosing: the act of picking or deciding between two or more possibilities; the opportunity or power to choose between two or more possibilities; the opportunity or power to make a decision.

Making Good Choices

It's so very important to make good choices. A good choice today will be reflected in your life at a later date in a positive way. A bad choice or decision you make today, you may have to live with for the rest of your life. Good choices today bring about good things for tomorrow. You must say what you mean and mean what you say when it comes to making choices. Don't allow others to influence you to do or say something that does not reflect who you really are.

I know the urge is there. You feel you are missing out on life. Well, if you can just WAIT, better things are coming your way! Besides, you are still growing as a young person. I know you don't want to be alone. I know it's just the thing to do. I know it's the grooviest thing to do! You want to be popular! You want to feel like somebody special! You are very special! You are your choice! I know! I know it feels like nobody understands you! Always be true to you and who you are!

Why are you in a hurry? Slow down! Get to know who you are before you hook up with someone and they tell you who you are. No one else can tell you who you are. You are who God says you are! Make good choices today for your tomorrow!

Be true to yourself! Be strong in what you believe! Read and be informed! You don't have to prove anything to anyone! Don't allow others to change your way of thinking! Seek God for wisdom even in this. God will give you wisdom and discernment to look to those close around you that show you love and kindness. They will help you in making good choices. When you receive good advice, always take heed to it. Don't allow yourself to be rebellious just because. Making good choices will take you a lot further in this life. You must choose today for what's best for your tomorrows! Choose to be respectful and give honor to whom it is due. You choose. Your choices will define and validate you!

Get to Know You

Spend some quality time with you! Enjoy spending time with you! Read to you! Enhance you! Get to know what you really like! Get to know what you want to do with your life! Get to know what makes you happy! Get to know what you stand for! Get to know you! Love you! Enjoy life and all its ups and downs. You have plenty of time to be grown.

Be the best that you can be at whatever task given you or you choose. Define yourself by the right standards that you set. Strive to be the best that you can be. There is greatest in you! The greatest in you is waiting on you to let it out. The greatness in you is right at your own finger tips. You must develop the greatness. Don't settle for less! You must reach and excel to your highest potential. Reach for the sky!

There is nothing that will hold you back but you! Do not settle especially when others try to tell you who or what you should do. You owe it to yourself to be the best that you can be! You owe it to yourself to obtain or achieve all that you can for you!

Don't allow yourself to be bound. If you become bound, you will need to seek God's help for release of the pressure that you feel bottled up inside of you. God will hear you and deliver you. He is a very present help in the time of trouble.

You must have discipline and consistency in everything you do! Discipline and consistency teaches you to have a code of behavior; the necessity of order in your life; how to follow direction; how to adhere to and follow rules and regulations; how to maintain control; helps you maintain an open mind to teaching and instructions; and respect those in authority.

Get to know the greatest that God put in you!

Integrity Is Key

You must stand for something! Know what you stand for or you will fall for anything. Stand up for what's right. Live a life that you can be proud of yourself and your accomplishments. Don't allow others to put you down. Know who you are. Do your best in all things. When you do your best, it doesn't matter what others say. When you do your best, you will have confidence in yourself. Always strive to be better than you were the last time.

Be confident enough in yourself that you set your standards and goals to something that really interests you so that it will encourage and inspire YOU to do your very best. Make long term goals but also make short term goals. Know that you can do all things through Christ. Make yourself a poster board, log or use a tablet to visualize your daily, week or monthly goals and accomplishments. Be confident! Be encouraged!

Speak good things over you! Love you! Love is great! Don't rush it! Don't allow others to take advantage of your love. Love and enjoy the fun but Wait for Adult Love when thinking of having a serious relationship with someone. Don't make adult decisions with a child's mind. Wait! Allow yourself to grow into an adult and then make adult decisions from an adult's perspective. Believe me as an adult you will see things totally different. Enjoy you now!

Always be honest and fair with others as well as yourself! Love everybody. Stand up for your morals. Don't allow others mistreatment of you to take your love from you. Remain who you are. You are whole! You are complete! You are unique.

When someone shows you the ugly side of themselves, you must remember it. Don't be so easily led! You must be alert to what is really being said to you! Be strong in your convictions! Stand up for you! Always be the best that you can be!

Time Is On Your Side

Time is on your side. Time to be a young person. Time to grow into the best you that you can be. Time to play games. Time to enjoy family and friends. Time to travel, if possible. Time to stop and smell the roses. Time to spend with friends. Time to be and do whatever good thing you want to do. Time to develop you! Time to allow you to grow into who God called you to be!

Time to learn about life and its ups and down. Time to just check out things for yourself. Time to enjoy being you. Time to encourage yourself! Time to love you! Time to find out who you are and what you want out of this life God gave you. Time to dream of a future that only you can imagine but it's in your power to work at it and succeed. The sky is the limit. Reach for it. You can do all things through Christ which strengthens you. Believe in you. Trust God to lead, guide and direct your paths.

Before you think of committing yourself to someone else, you should concentrate and work on you and how strong you can be by yourself. You must value yourself. If your value is only determined by others, you will always under value yourself.

You got time to just have fun! Time to excel at whatever task you strive for. Strive for the mastery. You can do it. Yes you can. Be the best that you can be!

You got time to get to know your family and friends. Always value your time with family. Look for ways to work together. Look for ways to improve your relationship with family and friends. Get to know the whole you!

The things you say and do while a child will be remembered even when you become an adult. Be quick to forgive. Don't allow things done to you to take hold of you or it will hold you back from being all you can be.

Your Purpose

Take time to find out your purpose in life. The purpose for which God created you. Your purpose was established even before the foundation of the world. Don't you want to get to know you while you have time to invest in you! While you have time to discover your inner self! To connect with you and your inner thoughts. To allow your creative thoughts to flourish into reality.

Know that your reality is what you make it. Things can become real really fast if you allow others to make decisions for you! Permanent repercussions will then dictate your life. The bible teaches us to "be careful for nothing". So that means you must listen, be watchful and prayerful so that you won't be so easily led or fooled by others. Your purpose will be lost if someone else dictates who you are and how you should feel. You must fulfil your purpose sooner or later, preferably sooner. You choose! You choose your plan and directions!

You Need Wisdom

As you mature, you need wisdom in everything you do. Just ask God for wisdom and He will freely give it to you! Wisdom gives you insight to people, problems, situations and You. Wisdom speaks to your heart to guide you! Wisdom is the key thing to have. Wisdom leads and guides you in the right direction. Wisdom teaches you! God gives us wisdom. From out of God's mouth comes knowledge and understanding. If you have wisdom, you will love your own soul and if you keep understanding, you shall find good.

You are wonderfully and fearfully made! You are a child of God and very special! You are one of a kind. You have a purpose that no one else can accomplish. You alone hold the key to life as you. You are a chosen vessel. You alone hold the key to your overall existence in this world. You are unique! You are special! You are more than a conqueror! You are victorious! Be wise! In all your getting, get understanding!

You Decide

You must decide which direction you want to take in life. You can be anything you want to be. Take some time to get to know you. Evaluate yourself. Don't allow yourself to be complacent. Being complacent keeps you focused on the here and now rather than on future goals. Complacency keeps you from wanting to improve or want better for yourself. Don't settle. If you are not where you want or need to be, then study to improve yourself. Take yourself seriously. You decide!

You only live once so why not enjoy your trip. Enjoy being a young lady or young man. You deserve it! Love you! Love the you that God chose you to be! You had no choice in how you look but everything to do with how you allow yourself to feel about things. You decide that you can be anything you want to be. You must decide who and what you want for you! You must choose to allow the greatest in you to come into fruiton. It your decision! You decide!

Know You

Don't allow anyone to pressure you into anything. You are the boss of you. It doesn't matter how many others are doing it, you stand up for you. You are responsible for you and your actions. You must let others know just how important your life is to you. You decide. There are people who like to dominate or be the boss of other people. They will try to tell you in no uncertain terms that you ought to do this or that. Trust you. Know you and what you want for you and don't allow anyone to tell you any difference. Maintain your morals!

Value yourself. Always know what's best for you and make a stand on it. Be sure of what's right for you and stand up for your right. Know of a surety that being you is the best thing in the world. Be true to you! When you have a relationship with God, He will direct your thoughts for your greater good that's in you. Be very sure of who you are and don't allow others to tell you who you are. There is greatness in You. Know you!

Know Who You Are

Don't be deceived, clothes don't make a person! It's what's inside that counts! You are who God says you are! You can be what God says you can be! Don't allow others to dictate your feelings. You have a right to your feelings. Believe in you. Know that your worth is not determined by what you wear! Know that you were born for greatness! You outgrow clothes and shoes! Shouldn't you be growing into the greatness that is in you! You are very important and have a lot to offer you and others. Know who you are and whose you are!

You are not defined by what you wear but you will be defined by the people you hang around with. Bad company causes you take on some bad habits. Always be very sure of who you are that others can't just pressure you into doing things just to get along with them. Don't go along just to get along. Stand up for you. God created You! You are great!

You

You had nothing to do with how you look but you have everything to do with how you feel about you; what you think about you; what you want for you; your future and your thoughts. When you spend time with you, in reading to you, to enhance you, it gives you a deeper understanding of just who you are or could be. The sky is the limit. Reach for it. It's up to you. You hold the key to you in your hand. Make a stand for you on what you will or will not tolerate.

Set your standards high. Why not? You are worth it. Set a goal for yourself and start planning and working on it. You are who you choose to be. Choose greatness for you. Choose to be happy. Love people not because of but in spite of what they may do. Forgive quickly! Unforgiveness hurts you in the long run. Learn from your mistakes and try not to repeat them. You are the best thing that ever happened to you! You are great! You are who God says you are! You are important!

You and School

When it comes to your school work, make sure you give you the best you have. Take time to study. Take time to research. Develop you. You deserve it! Read! Read! Read! It's very important for your development. Reading opens up roads to many ideas, suggestions, places and things to do. Your future is waiting on you to make good decisions for you and what you are expecting from you! You choose!

You must write your own life story and not allow others to write, dictate or validate who you are! Trust and believe in you! Take time with you in learning your school subjects. The subjects you learn when young will always be a part of you. You can look back on it later and say, hey I learned that in elementary school. Stay in touch with your development. It will make a difference later. If you pour knowledge into you now, it will help you later. Always seek to educate you!

You and God

God knew you even before you were in your Mother's womb. You have a calling on your life. You were born for greatness! You were called and chosen for a purpose that only you can fulfil. God has declared in His word that He has plans and thoughts of peace and not for evil to give you an expected end. God will perfect that which concerns you. His mercy endures forever. His compassion fails not.

If there are some things about you that you don't like, seek God and ask Him. He is as close as your heart throb.

Seek the kingdom of God and His righteousness and He will add all things that you need. Make some time to pray and read the Bible. If you want to know what God has to say about something, ask Him in prayer! He will answer your prayers!

You must have and maintain a personal relationship with God! It is the key to your development! Every good and perfect gift comes from above. Search for Him and you will find Him! If you remain in God, He will remain in you! If you believe and trust in Him, He will supply your every needs according to His divine will, way, plan and purpose for your life.

God loves us so much that He gave His only begotten son, Jesus, to die for us. God also said that if we walk upright that He would not withhold any good thing from us.

God loves you! He created you to be Victorious! You are more than a Conqueror! You are an Overcomer! You are who God says you are. You are Special. You are who God says you are!

A Feeling of Void in Your Life

If you feel you have a void in your life, you are vulnerable. Others will pick up on it because your actions and conversations will reflect it. You may try to fill that void with drugs, alcohol, sex and other people! All of these are temporary fixes and won't give you a feeling of total fulfilment! You must have a personal relationship with God. God will fill your void with love, joy, peace, happiness, etc.

If you feel you have a void or emptiness inside of you, you will feel the need to fill it! You are now vulnerable and now you are set-up for failure! Other people will try to tell you who you are or try to define you! They will try to tell you what and how you should do things and even how you should feel about somethings! You are lost when you allow others to think for you! You must maintain a personal relationship with God. God can fill your emptiness and void if you open up your heart and let Him come into your life.

When You are disconnected from the source and the vine, who is Christ, things just won't seem to work out! Christ can and will fill any void in your life! Seek Him first and He will add to you whatever you are in need of in this life! We are the branches and we cannot survive unless we are connected to the vine! Jesus is the vine!

Don't allow others to define, validate, direct or manipulate you into being someone you are not! You are who God says you are! You are His possession! He bought us on Calvary Cross! He freed us not to be bound again to the cares of this world!

To thine own self be true! Seek God while He may be found. Call upon Him while He is yet near. He loves and cares about you! You will never feel alone for God said He would never leave us nor forsake us! He will remain with you if you remain with Him. He said He will supply your every needs!

Don't Be Fooled

If someone is rude and disrespectful to somebody else for no reason, don't think that you are so special! In time, they will show you who they really are. Believe them! In time, they will be rude to you and you will be disrespected as well! Don't be fooled by the smooth words but listen and pay attention to the actions! Actions speak louder than words! Don't be fooled by what a person says but be alert to their actions.

God can change anybody! A person no matter how special that they think they are cannot change another person. If so, it's only temporary! A person must sincerely want to be changed and seek God and He will change them! God is the only one that can change man or woman's heart (Psalm 51:10) if they seek Him first and His righteousness! Seek God's wisdom in all things. He will lead, guide and direct you!

Summary

In Summary, I have tried to give insight to different areas of life that a child may encounter. Most of my insights come from my relationship with God and the many years of working with children. I've tried to be specific about things that they have shared with me. I hope this book will help in development and enhancement. May God bless you, lead and guide you in your future thoughts, goals and development.

To God be all the glory in all things!

Sources of References

King James Bible

Insights – From over 50 years of experience with children,

Made in the USA
Columbia, SC
27 April 2024